Lamaste

AF390971

This Gratitude Journal

Belongs to :

____

Special Request

Dear customers,

Thank you for your trust.

I'm an independent publisher.

If you like this journal, feel free to follow my

work on my website : www.olindavida.com

so you don't miss any update.

I hope you will enjoy this journal as much as I

enjoyed designing it !

Erika Rossi
- Ô LINDA VIDA -

Thank you very much in advance !

Lamaste - Gratitude Journal for Kids

© Copyright 2020 by Erika Rossi. All Rights Reserved.
This publication is protected by copyright and may not be reproduced without the author's written consent.

Note to Parents

About gratitude….

Gratitude invites us to focus on what we have, rather than what we lack. It is not an innate skill, it is learned. Cultivating joy and gratitude is therefore an important habit to establish from a young age. It has been scientifically proven that gratitude has a beneficial effect on health (both physical and mental) in addition to allowing us to maintain better relationships with others, and plays an essential role in our happiness. Keeping a gratitude diary allows us to adopt a positive ritual and to anchor this habit in our daily life and in the long term. By becoming aware of our emotions and the treasures we already possess (abilities as well as relationships), we increase our capital of self-confidence and confidence in life.

How to use this diary

Ideally, this diary should be filled in daily for a few minutes, as habits are forged by regularity. However, it is important to avoid making it an obligation. If your child wants to skip one day, that's okay, writing should not become a chore but remain a fun activity.

Above all, this journal is a personal tool and a privileged means of expression for your child. If they are still too young to read and keep the diary alone, you can do this activity together. If they are old enough to be independent, offer for them to share their writings with you, if that is their wish. You can also share more generally about the positive elements of their day, which can be the starting point for enriching conversations. If you like the idea of a journal, you can also start your own. Indeed, the best way to convey gratitude to children is probably to set an example by cultivating this healthy attitude ourselves.

Composition of the Diary

This journal contains 111 pages, including more than 90 days of practice (91 days for 13 weeks) and 13 pages of weekly activities (one page following 7 consecutive days of practice). According to studies concerning the neuroplasticity of our brains, 90 days are necessary to anchor a new habit.

Each practice page includes the date to be completed, the mood of the day to be circled, the three things your child feels grateful for, the best time of day, the person who brought them joy, the things that excite them for the next day and an "inspiring quote", "positive affirmation" or "challenge of the day" that changes every day. This last part adds a touch of novelty while combining well with the repetitive and relatively short nature of the other exercises, providing reassuring benchmarks and helping to keep the child motivated.

Quotes, Affirmations & Challenges

Inspirational quotes allow your child to reflect on different concepts while continuing to motivate them. Some sentences may be more complex for your child to grasp depending on their age, so don't hesitate to discuss those with them and adjust the most difficult ones with more targeted examples.

The purpose of positive affirmations is to offer mantras, positive benchmarks for your child that can be repeated and/or written several times in order to better absorb them and integrate them as personal truths (through self-suggestion). They are ideal for building self-confidence.

The daily challenges allow your child to take actions in their daily life that are beneficial to those around them as well as to themselves, to take full advantage of the effects of gratitude and to cultivate more joy.

Note to the Child

What is Gratitude ?

This journal is just for you. If you fill it out regularly (it's best to write in it every day, but if you miss a few times it's okay), it's like planting seeds in your garden to cultivate what is called "gratitude". These are seeds that will grow little by little to help you feel more grateful for everything you already have in your life, and to think less about what you might be missing. More gratitude makes you feel better, both in body and mind. It's like becoming the gardener of your secret garden and reaping the fruits of your own happiness !

How to use your Journal

Settle down in a quiet place where you will feel comfortable to think and fill out your journal. You can write in your journal, but you can also personalise it by decorating it, sticking stickers or colouring it to your taste! You can choose to keep what you write to yourself or share it with your parents if you feel like it. Don't hesitate to ask an adult if some sentences are hard to understand.

Loris the Lama will be present with you throughout the Journal, he is a master of Gratitude, you can count on him! Cheese the Cat will help you to identify your mood of the day. You have one page to fill each day with a quote or a small challenge to achieve each time. Inspiring quotes are here to make you think about great things in life. You can read Positive Affirmations, think about their meaning and repeat them, their goal is to make you feel better about yourself and more confident. If you can't do the challenge on the same day, it doesn't matter, just do it whenever you can. After seven days, you will have another fun activity to do.

Enjoy your « Happiness Gardening »!

We already filled in a page as an example for you :

Date : **M T W T F S**

★ _15_ / _10_ / _2020_

Today I feel : (Circle one)

3 Things I am Thankful for :

My toys

My best friend Sean

Nature

The Best Time
of my Day : (Draw or Write)

When Dad and I walked in the woods after school.

Tomorrow will be Great because :

I'll receive my new magazine

I'll see Aunty

This Person
brought me joy :

Mom

Inspiring Quote

« A Thankful Heart is a Happy Heart. »

Date :   M T W T F S D
★   __ / __ / ____

Today I feel : (Circle one)

3 Things I am Thankful for :

The Best Time
of my Day :   (Draw or Write)

This Person
brought me joy :

Tomorrow will be
Great because :

Inspiring Quote
« A Thankful Heart is a
Happy Heart. »

Date :
M T W T F S D
__ / __ / ____
Today I feel : (Circle one)
3 Things I am Thankful for :
The Best Time
of my Day :   (Draw or Write)
Tomorrow will be Great because :
This Person
brought me joy :
Positive Affirmation
« I've got everything I need. »

Date :
M T W T F S D
__ / __ / ____
Today I feel : (Circle one)
3 Things I am Thankful for :
The Best Time of my Day : (Draw or Write)
Tomorrow will be Great because :
This Person brought me joy :
Kindness Challenge
Write down three things you like about one of your parents and give them the paper.

Date : **M T W T F S D**

★ __ / __ / ____

3 Things I am Thankful for :

★

The Best Time of my Day : (Draw or Write)

Tomorrow will be Great because :

This Person brought me joy :

Inspiring Quote

« To be courageous is knowing fear but still facing it. »

Date : **M T W T F S D**

★ __ / __ / ____

3 Things I am Thankful for :

★

Tomorrow will be Great because :

★

This Person brought me joy :

Positive Affirmation

« Mistakes are part of success, I have the right to make mistakes. »

★

Date :   **M T W T F S D**

★   __ / __ / ____

Today I feel : (Circle one)

3 Things I am Thankful for :

The Best Time
of my Day :   (Draw or Write)

Tomorrow will be Great because :

This Person
brought me joy :

Happiness Challenge
Choose a place in your room to display the drawing or photo of someone you love.

Date :   M T W T F S D
★   __ / __ / ____

Today I feel : (Circle one)

3 Things I am Thankful for :

The Best Time
of my Day :   (Draw or Write)

Tomorrow will be
Great because :

This Person
brought me joy :

Inspiring Quote
« True Friendship is a
treasure. »

Objective : Gratitude !

Activity

Write down 5 things that always make you smile.

1

2

3

OH HAPPY DAY

4

5

Date : **M T W T F S D**

★ __ / __ / ____

Today I feel : (Circle one)

3 Things I am Thankful for :

★

The Best Time
of my Day :   (Draw or Write)

Tomorrow will be Great because :

★

This Person
brought me joy :

Positive Affirmation

« I have the right to be different from others. »

Date : **M T W T F S D**

★ __ / __ / ____

Today I feel : (Circle one)

3 Things I am Thankful for :

The Best Time of my Day : (Draw or Write)

Tomorrow will be Great because :

This Person brought me joy :

Inspiring Quote

« A smile dispels many worries. »

- Chinese proverb -

Date :
M T W T F S D
__ / __ / ____
Today I feel : (Circle one)
3 Things I am Thankful for :
The Best Time
of my Day :   (Draw or Write)
Tomorrow will be Great because :
This Person
brought me joy :
Kindness Challenge
Think of someone you don't like and try to find two qualities in them.

Date : **M T W T F S D**

★ __ / __ / ____

Today I feel : (Circle one)

3 Things I am Thankful for :

★

★

The Best Time
of my Day :   (Draw or Write)

Tomorrow will be Great because :

★

This Person
brought me joy :

Positive Affirmation

« There is always someone who thinks about me and loves me. »

Date: M T W T F S D

★ __ / __ / ____

Today I feel : (Circle one)

3 Things I am Thankful for :

★

The Best Time
of my Day :   (Draw or Write)

Tomorrow will be Great because :

★

This Person brought me joy :

Inspiring Quote
« Be the friend you want to have. »

Date :
M T W T F S D
__ / __ / ____

Today I feel : (Circle one)

3 Things I am Thankful for :

The Best Time
of my Day :   (Draw or Write)

Tomorrow will be
Great because :

This Person
brought me joy :

Kindness Challenge
Offer a drawing to
someone.

Date :   M T W T F S D
★ __ / __ / ____
Today I feel : (Circle one)
3 Things I am Thankful for :
The Best Time
of my Day :   (Draw or Write)
Tomorrow will be Great because :
This Person
brought me joy :
Positive Affirmation
«I am capable: I have the resources within me to succeed.»

Take a walk in a park, a square or a forest.

Take the time to use your different senses: for example, you can admire the birds, enjoy the sensation of the sun on your skin, smell the flowers or listen to the sounds made by the people and vehicles around you.

How lucky are we to be alive and to be able to do all these things !

Write down what you liked best about this walk:

____

____

____

____

Date : **M T W T F S D**

★ __ / __ / ____

Today I feel : (Circle one)

3 Things I am Thankful for :

★

Tomorrow will be Great because :

The Best Time
of my Day :   (Draw or Write)

This Person
brought me joy :

Inspiring Quote

« Only those who do nothing never make a mistake. »
- African proverb -

Date :   **M T W T F S D**

★   __ / __ / ____

Today *I feel* : (Circle one)

3 Things *I am Thankful for* :

The Best Time
of my Day :   (Draw or Write)

Tomorrow will be Great *because* :

This Person
brought me joy :

Kindness Challenge
Write down 3 things you
like about another parent
and give him/her the
paper.

Date : **M T W T F S D**

★ __ / __ / ____

Today I feel : (Circle one)

3 Things I am Thankful for :

The Best Time
of my Day :   (Draw or Write)

Tomorrow will be Great because :

This Person
brought me joy :

Positive Affirmation
« I have the right to ask, give, receive and refuse. »

Date : **M T W T F S D**

★ __ / __ / ____

Today I feel : (Circle one)

3 Things I am Thankful for :

The Best Time
of my Day :   (Draw or Write)

Tomorrow will be Great because :

This Person
brought me joy :

Inspiring Quote

"Life isn't about waiting for the storm to pass. It's about learning how to dance in the rain."
- Sénèque -

Date :
M T W T F S D
__ / __ / ____
Today I feel : (Circle one)
3 Things I am Thankful for :
The Best Time
of my Day :   (Draw or Write)
Tomorrow will be Great because :
This Person
brought me joy :
Kindness Challenge
Tell a funny story to someone who seems bored or sad.

Date : M T W T F S D
__ / __ / ____

Today I feel : (Circle one)

3 Things I am Thankful for :

The Best Time
of my Day : (Draw or Write)

Tomorrow will be
Great because :

This Person
brought me joy :

Positive Affirmation
« I have as much value as
others. »

Date : **M T W T F S D**

★ __ / __ /____

Today I feel : (Circle one)

3 Things I am Thankful for :

The Best Time
of my Day :   (Draw or Write)

Tomorrow will be Great because :

This Person
brought me joy :

Inspiring Quote
"When you arise in the morning, think of what a precious privilege it is to be alive-to breathe, to think, to enjoy, to love."
- Marcus Aurelius -

Objective : Gratitude !

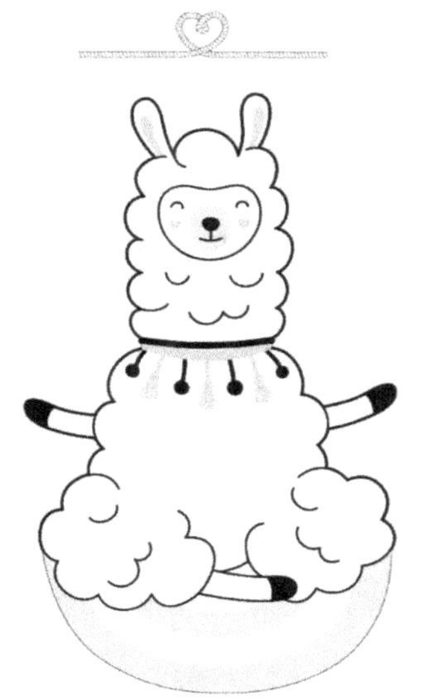

Activity

Gratitude Letter

Write a letter to thank someone who has done something nice for you and offer it to them.

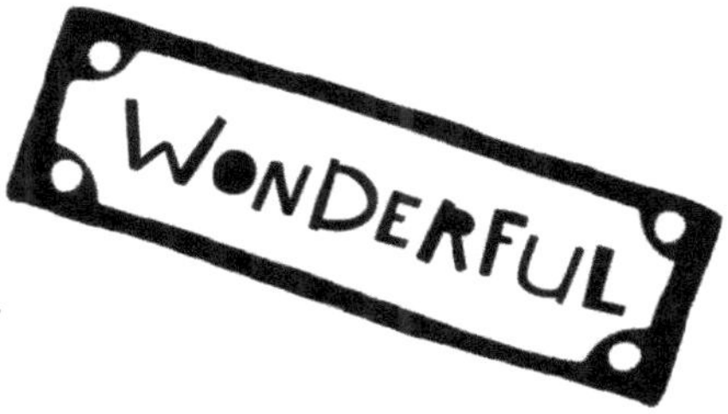

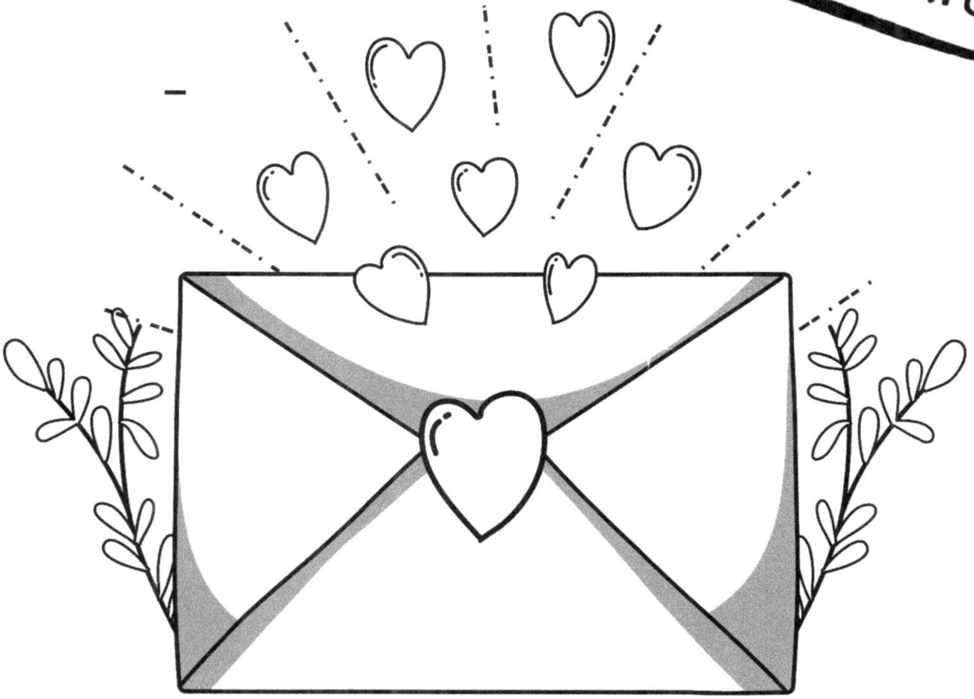

Date :
M T W T F S D
__ / __ / ____
Today I feel : (Circle one)
3 Things I am Thankful for :
The Best Time
of my Day :   (Draw or Write)
Tomorrow will be Great because :
This Person
brought me joy :
Kindness Challenge
« Name 3 people you are happy to know. »

Date :   M T W T F S D
__ / __ / ____

Today I feel : (Circle one)

3 Things I am Thankful for :

The Best Time
of my Day :   (Draw or Write)

Tomorrow will be
Great because :

This Person
brought me joy :

Positive Affirmation
« I can dream and pursue
my dreams. »

Date : **M T W T F S D**

★ __ / __ / ____

Today I feel : (Circle one)

3 Things I am Thankful for :

The Best Time
of my Day :   (Draw or Write)

Tomorrow will be Great because :

This Person
brought me joy :

Inspiring Quote

"It's important to make mistakes in order to learn: making mistakes is part of learning."

Date : **M T W T F S D**

★ __ / __ / ____

Today I feel : (Circle one)

3 Things I am Thankful for :

★

The Best Time
of my Day :   (Draw or Write)

★

Tomorrow will be Great because :

★

This Person
brought me joy :

Kindness Challenge

« Smile to someone with all your kindness. »

Date : **M T W T F S D**

★ __ / __ / ____

Today I feel : (Circle one)

3 Things I am Thankful for :

The Best Time
of my Day :   (Draw or Write)

Tomorrow will be Great because :

This Person
brought me joy :

Positive Affirmation

« I have the right to express my emotions. »

Date : **M T W T F S D**

★ __ / __ / ____

Today I feel : (Circle one)

3 Things I am Thankful for :

The Best Time
of my Day :   (Draw or Write)

Tomorrow will be Great because :

This Person
brought me joy :

Inspiring Quote

« Be kind to others without expecting anything in return. »

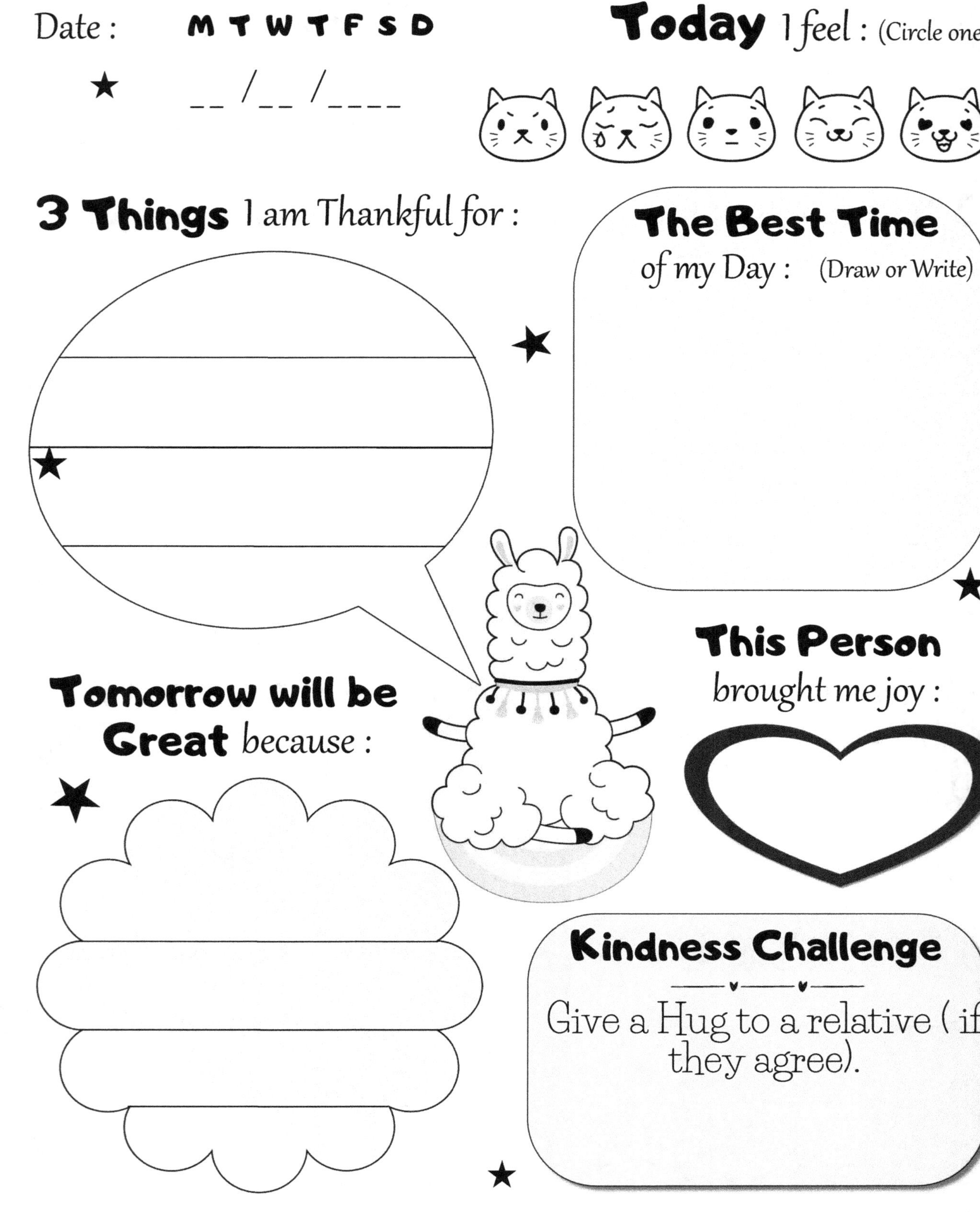

Date :   M T W T F S D
__ / __ / ____
Today I feel : (Circle one)
3 Things I am Thankful for :
The Best Time of my Day :   (Draw or Write)
Tomorrow will be Great because :
This Person brought me joy :
Kindness Challenge
Give a Hug to a relative (if they agree).

Objective : Gratitude !

Activity

Draw in the frame the people you

love the most !

Date : **M T W T F S D**

★ __ / __ / ____

Today I feel : (Circle one)

Date :　　M T W T F S D

★　　__ / __ / ____

Today I feel : (Circle one)

3 Things I am Thankful for :

★

The Best Time
of my Day :　(Draw or Write)

Tomorrow will be Great because :

This Person brought me joy :

Inspiring Quote

"It does not matter how slowly you go, as long as you don't stop".

- Confucius -

Date : **M T W T F S D**

★ __ / __ /____

Today I feel : (Circle one)

3 Things I am Thankful for :

The Best Time of my Day : (Draw or Write)

Tomorrow will be Great because :

This Person brought me joy :

Kindness Challenge

Help your parents make dinner.

Date :   M T W T F S D

★   __ / __ / ____

Today I feel : (Circle one)

3 Things I am Thankful for :

★

The Best Time
of my Day :   (Draw or Write)

Tomorrow will be Great because :

★

This Person
brought me joy :

Positive Affirmation
« I am beautiful and perfect the way I am. »

Date : M T W T F S D

★ __ / __ / ____

Today I feel : (Circle one)

3 Things I am Thankful for :

★

The Best Time
of my Day : (Draw or Write)

Tomorrow will be Great because :

★

This Person brought me joy :

Inspiring Quote

« Your body is your home:
take care of it. »

Date :
M T W T F S D
__ / __ / ___
Today I feel : (Circle one)
3 Things I am Thankful for :
The Best Time
of my Day :   (Draw or Write)
Tomorrow will be Great because :
This Person brought me joy :
Kindness Challenge
Write to a friend what you like best about them.

Date :
M T W T F S D
__ / __ / ____
Today I feel : (Circle one)
3 Things I am Thankful for :
The Best Time
of my Day :   (Draw or Write)
Tomorrow will be Great because :
This Person
brought me joy :
Positive Affirmation
« I am important. »

Circle the things that make you grateful :

My Body

My Home

My Bedroom

Nature

My Parents

My Dog

Sunshine   My Brother

My Garden

My Cat   My Friends

My Books

My Bike

Hot Chocolate

My cousins   My School

My Neighbors   My Toys

MADE WITH LOVE

Date : **M T W T F S D**
★ __ / __ / ____

Today I feel : (Circle one)

3 Things I am Thankful for :

★

The Best Time
of my Day :   (Draw or Write)

Tomorrow will be Great because :

This Person
brought me joy :

Inspiring Quote

« Think about everything you've already achieved and smile. »

Date :
M T W T F S D
★   __ / __ / ____

Today I feel : (Circle one)

3 Things I am Thankful for :

The Best Time
of my Day :   (Draw or Write)

Tomorrow will be
Great because :

This Person
brought me joy :

Kindness Challenge
Offer help to someone
without being asked for it.

Date :
M T W T F S D
__ / __ / ____
Today I feel : (Circle one)
3 Things I am Thankful for :
The Best Time
of my Day :   (Draw or Write)
Tomorrow will be Great because :
This Person
brought me joy :
Positive Affirmation
« I am allowed to take up space. »

Date :
M T W T F S D
__ / __ / __
Today I feel : (Circle one)
3 Things I am Thankful for :
The Best Time
of my Day :   (Draw or Write)
Tomorrow will be Great because :
This Person
brought me joy :
Inspiring Quote
"The best time to plant a tree was 20 years ago. The second best time is now." - Chinese proverb -

Date : M T W T F S D

★ __ / __ / ____

Today I feel : (Circle one)

3 Things I am Thankful for :

The Best Time
of my Day :   (Draw or Write)

Tomorrow will be Great because :

This Person
brought me joy :

Kindness Challenge

Answer these questions:
« Who did you help today? Who could you help tomorrow? »

Date :
M T W T F S D
__ / __ / ____
Today I feel : (Circle one)
3 Things I am Thankful for :
The Best Time
of my Day :   (Draw or Write)
Tomorrow will be
Great because :
This Person
brought me joy :
Positive Affirmation
« I am Unique. »

Date : **M T W T F S D**
★ __ / __ / ____

Today I feel : (Circle one)

3 Things I am Thankful for :

The Best Time
of my Day :   (Draw or Write)

Tomorrow will be Great because :

This Person
brought me joy :

Inspiring Quote
"The wise man thinks before he acts."

- Persian proverb -

What did you learn this week?

Write down three things and read what you wrote. Be proud of yourself and be thankful that you learned so much!

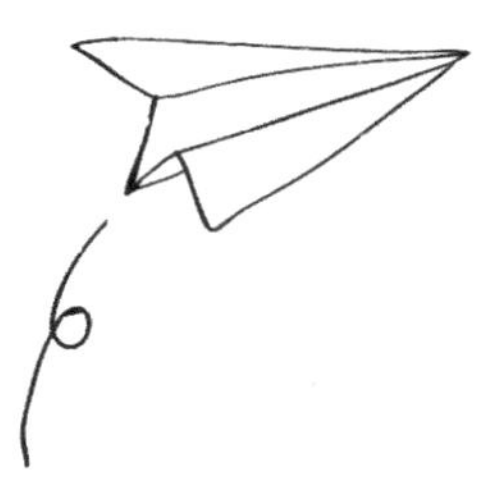

1 ____

2 ____

3 ____

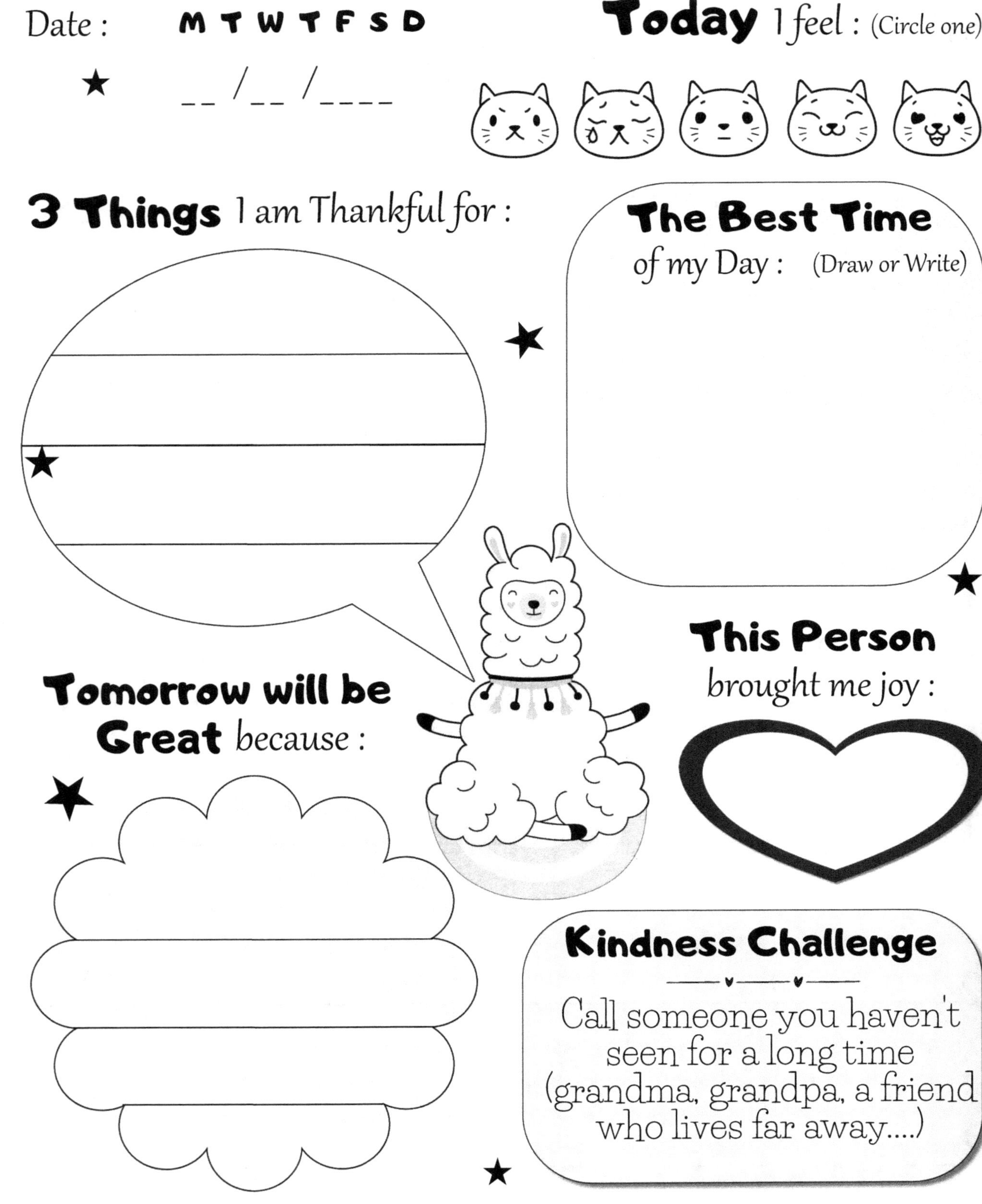

Date :   M T W T F S D
__ / __ / ____

Today I feel : (Circle one)

3 Things I am Thankful for :

The Best Time
of my Day :   (Draw or Write)

Tomorrow will be Great because :

This Person
brought me joy :

Kindness Challenge
Call someone you haven't seen for a long time (grandma, grandpa, a friend who lives far away....)

Date : **M T W T F S D**

★ __ / __ / ____

Today I feel : (Circle one)

3 Things I am Thankful for :

★

The Best Time
of my Day :   (Draw or Write)

Tomorrow will be Great because :

★

This Person
brought me joy :

Positive Affirmation

« I have the power to help others. »

Date :
M T W T F S D
__ / __ / ____
Today I feel : (Circle one)
3 Things I am Thankful for :
The Best Time
of my Day :   (Draw or Write)
This Person
brought me joy :
Tomorrow will be
Great because :
Inspiring Quote
"Alone we go faster,
together we go further."
- African proverb -

Date :
M T W T F S D
__ / __ / ____

Today I feel : (Circle one)

3 Things I am Thankful for :

The Best Time
of my Day :   (Draw or Write)

Tomorrow will be
Great because :

This Person
brought me joy :

Kindness Challenge
At your next meal, think about all the people who have worked so that you can eat this food and talk about it with your family.

Date :   **M T W T F S D**

★   __ / __ / ____

3 Things I am Thankful for :

The Best Time
of my Day :   (Draw or Write)

★

Tomorrow will be Great because :

★

This Person
brought me joy :

Positive Affirmation

"I am capable of inventing great things. »

★

Date :   M T W T F S D
★   __ / __ / ____

Today I feel : (Circle one)

3 Things I am Thankful for :

The Best Time
of my Day :   (Draw or Write)

Tomorrow will be
Great because :

This Person
brought me joy :

Inspiring Quote
« He who is contented is rich. »
- Lao-Tseu -

Date : M T W T F S D
__ / __ / ____

Today I feel : (Circle one)

3 Things I am Thankful for :

The Best Time
of my Day :   (Draw or Write)

Tomorrow will be
Great because :

This Person
brought me joy :

Kindness Challenge
Advise or lend a book/
movie you liked to a friend
(with the agreement of
your parents).

Objective : Gratitude !

Activity

Draw an activity you like to do that gives you joy.

CHOOSE HAPPY

Date :   M T W T F S D
__ / __ / ____
Today I feel : (Circle one)
3 Things I am Thankful for :
The Best Time
of my Day :   (Draw or Write)
Tomorrow will be
Great because :
This Person
brought me joy :
Positive Affirmation
« My words matter. »

Date :
M T W T F S D
__ / __ / ____
Today I feel : (Circle one)
3 Things I am Thankful for :
The Best Time
of my Day :   (Draw or Write)
Tomorrow will be Great because :
This Person
brought me joy :
Inspiring Quote
"There are always several ways of expressing things: the wisest is the one that doesn't hurt anyone. "

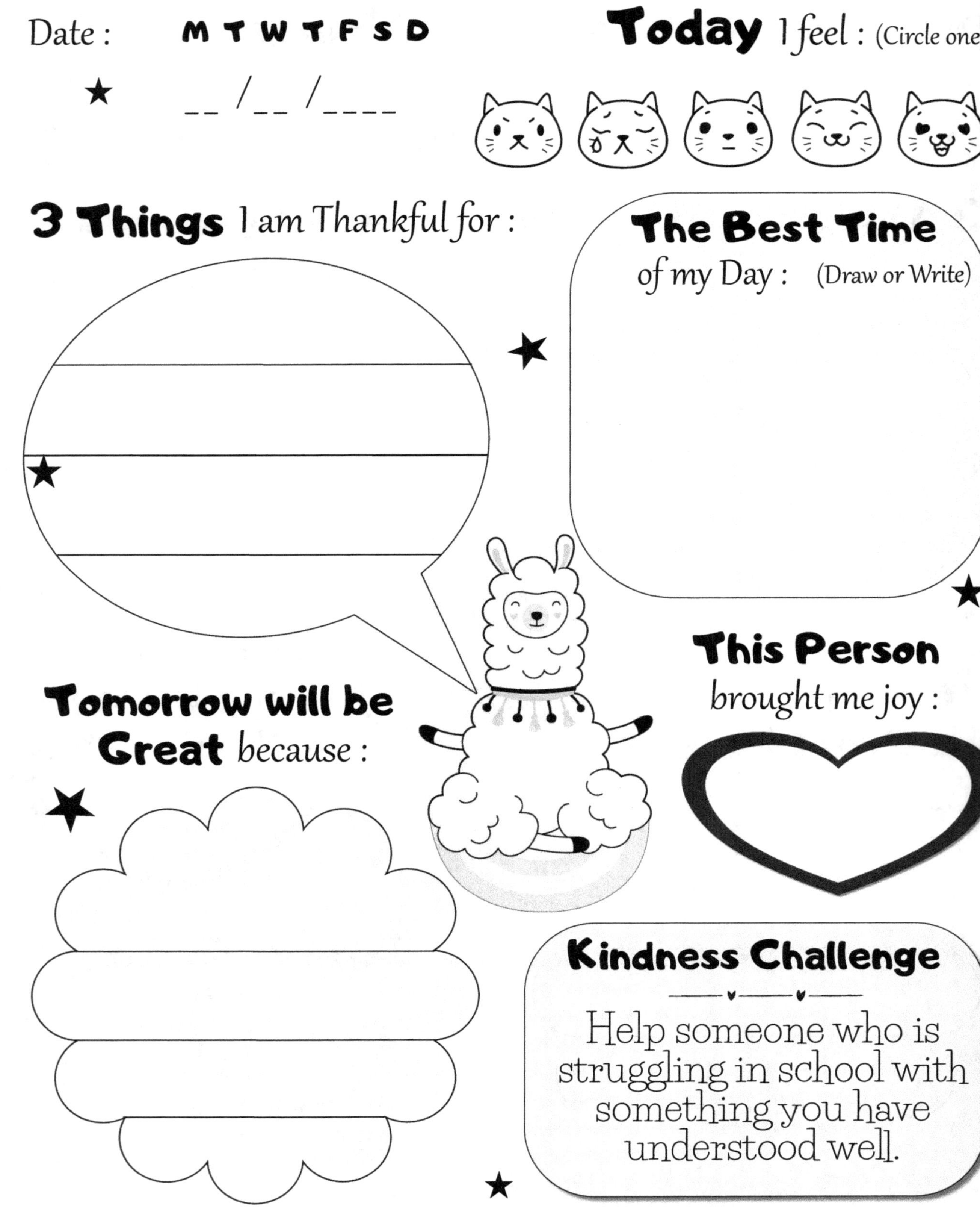

Date :
M T W T F S D
__ / __ / ____
Today I feel : (Circle one)
3 Things I am Thankful for :
The Best Time
of my Day :   (Draw or Write)
Tomorrow will be Great because :
This Person
brought me joy :
Kindness Challenge
Help someone who is struggling in school with something you have understood well.

Date :   M T W T F S D
★   __ / __ / ____
Today I feel : (Circle one)
3 Things I am Thankful for :
★
The Best Time
of my Day :   (Draw or Write)
This Person
brought me joy :
Tomorrow will be
Great because :
★
Positive Affirmation
"I've already accomplished
several feats such as
learning to walk, read, ride
a bike. »

Date : **M T W T F S D**

★ __ / __ / ____

Today I feel : (Circle one)

3 Things I am Thankful for :

The Best Time
of my Day :   (Draw or Write)

Tomorrow will be Great because :

This Person
brought me joy :

Inspiring Quote_

"You can always offer a smile or a encouragement to someone, it's free and the stock is unlimited."

Date : **M T W T F S D**

★ _ _ / _ _ / _ _ _ _

Today I feel : (Circle one)

3 Things I am Thankful for :

The Best Time
of my Day : (Draw or Write)

Tomorrow will be Great because :

This Person
brought me joy :

Kindness Challenge

Make a bracelet and offer it to a friend in sign of friendship.

Date :   M T W T F S D
__ / __ / ____

Today I feel : (Circle one)

3 Things I am Thankful for :

The Best Time
of my Day :   (Draw or Write)

Tomorrow will be
Great because :

This Person
brought me joy :

Positive Affirmation
"What I feel deserves to be
expressed. »

Activity

Imagine and write down your ideal day where you could do anything you wanted. What activities would you do and with whom ? Where would you go?

Date :   M T W T F S D
__ / __ / ____

Today I feel : (Circle one)

3 Things I am Thankful for :

The Best Time
of my Day :   (Draw or Write)

Tomorrow will be
Great because :

This Person
brought me joy :

Inspiring Quote
"Every day that begins is a
new chance to learn. »

Date :   M T W T F S D
__ / __ / ____

Today I feel : (Circle one)

3 Things I am Thankful for :

The Best Time
of my Day :   (Draw or Write)

Tomorrow will be
Great because :

This Person
brought me joy :

Kindness Challenge
Ask a person close to you
how they are doing and
listens to them.

Date :   M T W T F S D
__ / __ / ____
Today I feel : (Circle one)
3 Things I am Thankful for :
The Best Time of my Day :   (Draw or Write)
Tomorrow will be Great because :
This Person brought me joy :
Positive Affirmation
"I have the right to cry. »

Date :
M T W T F S D
__ / __ / ____
Today I feel : (Circle one)
3 Things I am Thankful for :
The Best Time of my Day : (Draw or Write)
Tomorrow will be Great because :
This Person brought me joy :
Inspiring Quote
« Love cannot be divided, it multiplies. »

Date :   M T W T F S D
★   __ / __ / ____
Today I feel : (Circle one)
3 Things I am Thankful for :
The Best Time
of my Day :   (Draw or Write)
Tomorrow will be Great because :
This Person
brought me joy :
Kindness Challenge
Ask a parent about the things they are grateful for in they life.

Date : **M T W T F S D**
★   __ / __ / ____

Today I feel : (Circle one)

3 Things I am Thankful for :

The Best Time
of my Day :   (Draw or Write)

Tomorrow will be Great because :

This Person
brought me joy :

Positive Affirmation
"When I breathe deeply, I feel soothed. »

Date : **M T W T F S D**

★ __ / __ / ____

Today I feel : (Circle one)

3 Things I am Thankful for :

The Best Time
of my Day : (Draw or Write)

Tomorrow will be Great because :

This Person
brought me joy :

Inspiring Quote

« The more we train, the more we improve. »

Write down what you like and admire most about your favorite hero / heroine from a movie, book or cartoon.

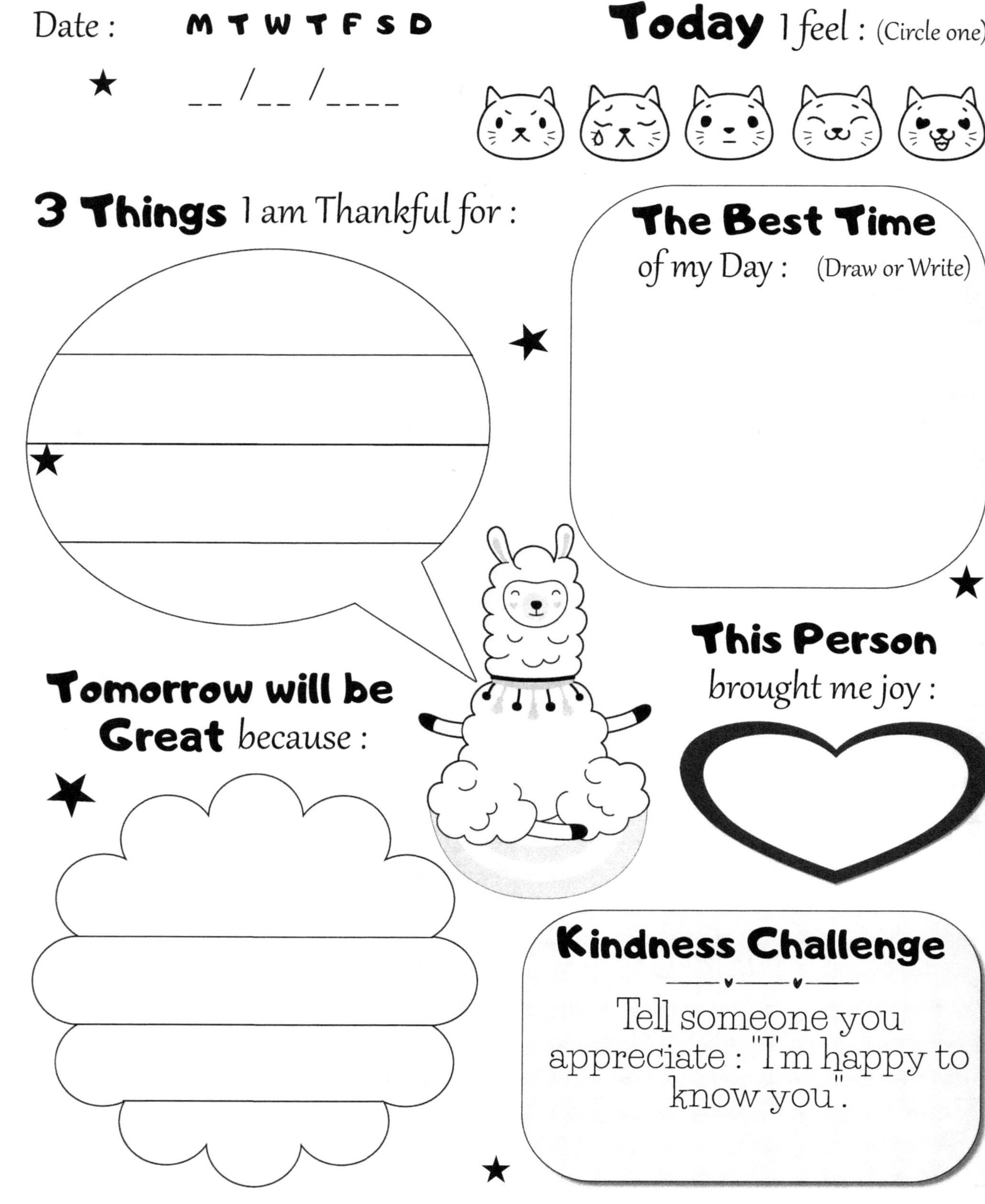

Date : **M T W T F S D**

★ __ / __ / ____

Today I feel : (Circle one)

3 Things I am Thankful for :

The Best Time
of my Day : (Draw or Write)

Tomorrow will be Great because :

This Person
brought me joy :

Kindness Challenge

Tell someone you appreciate : "I'm happy to know you".

Date :
M T W T F S D
__ / __ / ____
Today I feel : (Circle one)
3 Things I am Thankful for :
The Best Time
of my Day :   (Draw or Write)
Tomorrow will be Great because :
This Person
brought me joy :
Positive Affirmation
« I deserve to be happy. »

Date : **M T W T F S D**

★ __ / __ / ____

3 Things I am Thankful for :

★

The Best Time
of my Day :   (Draw or Write)

Tomorrow will be Great because :

★

This Person
brought me joy :

Inspiring Quote

« Imagination is a muscle that develops by using it. »

Date :   M T W T F S D
__ / __ / ____

Today I feel : (Circle one)

3 Things I am Thankful for :

The Best Time
of my Day :   (Draw or Write)

This Person
brought me joy :

Tomorrow will be
Great because :

Kindness Challenge
Find something nice to tell
someone that you don't
know well (about their
clothes, their hairstyle
etc).

Date :   M T W T F S D
__ / __ / ____

Today I feel : (Circle one)

3 Things I am Thankful for :

The Best Time
of my Day :   (Draw or Write)

Tomorrow will be
Great because :

This Person
brought me joy :

Positive Affirmation
« I express my gratitude
and my gratefulness
towards others. »

Date :
M T W T F S D
__ / __ / ____
Today I feel : (Circle one)
3 Things I am Thankful for :
The Best Time
of my Day :   (Draw or Write)
Tomorrow will be Great because :
This Person
brought me joy :
Inspiring Quote
« All work bears its fruits. »

Date : **M T W T F S D**
★ __ / __ / ____

Today I feel : (Circle one)

3 Things I am Thankful for :

The Best Time
of my Day :   (Draw or Write)

Tomorrow will be Great because :

This Person
brought me joy :

Happiness Challenge
Complete this sentence :
"I'm lucky because
______________________ »

Activity

Circle everything you are able to do. There must be a lot of them! Think for a few minutes about how lucky you are to be able to do all these things.

SPEAKING

GOING TO SCHOOL

COUNTING

RUNNING

LEARNING

SEEING

BICYCLE RIDING

SLEEPING IN A BED

WALKING

PLAYING

READING

WRITING

DRIVING

SMELLING

BREATHING

DREAMING

EATING EVERYDAY

LISTENING

LAUGHING

Date : **M T W T F S D**

★ __ / __ / ____

Today I feel : (Circle one)

3 Things I am Thankful for :

The Best Time
of my Day :   (Draw or Write)

Tomorrow will be Great because :

This Person
brought me joy :

Positive Affirmation

« Fear is a normal feeling. It decreases when I take an interest in it and make it my friend. »

Date :

M T W T F S D

★ __ / __ / ____

Today I feel : (Circle one)

3 Things I am Thankful for :

★

The Best Time
of my Day :   (Draw or Write)

Tomorrow will be Great because :

★

This Person
brought me joy :

Inspiring Quote

"You shouldn't be afraid of failing, but of not trying. »

Date :
M T W T F S D
__ / __ / ____
Today I feel : (Circle one)
3 Things I am Thankful for :
The Best Time
of my Day :   (Draw or Write)
Tomorrow will be Great because :
This Person brought me joy :
Happiness Challenge
« Close your eyes and imagine a sun smiling in your heart. Breathe deeply 3 times thinking about this sun. »

Date :
M T W T F S D
__ / __ / ____

Today I feel : (Circle one)

3 Things I am Thankful for :

The Best Time
of my Day :   (Draw or Write)

Tomorrow will be
Great because :

This Person
brought me joy :

Positive Affirmation
"Talking with others
enriches me."

Date : **M T W T F S D**

★ __ / __ / ____

Today *I feel :* (Circle one)

3 Things *I am Thankful for :*

The Best Time
of my Day :   (Draw or Write)

Tomorrow will be Great *because :*

This Person
brought me joy :

Inspiring Quote

« Our greatest glory is not in never falling, but in rising every time we fall. »

- Confucius -

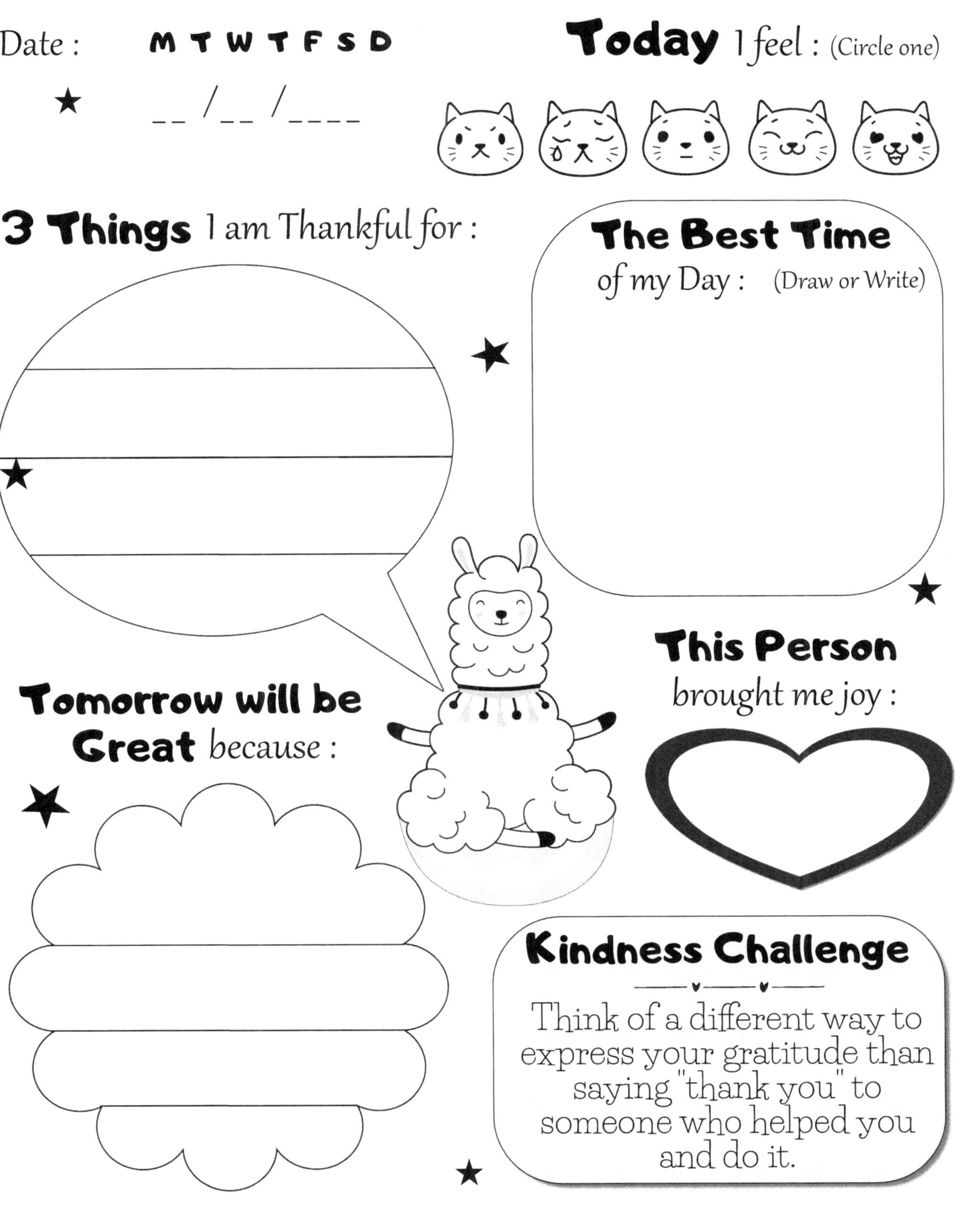

Date :
M T W T F S D
__ / __ / ____
Today I feel : (Circle one)
3 Things I am Thankful for :
The Best Time
of my Day :   (Draw or Write)
This Person
brought me joy :
Tomorrow will be
Great because :
Kindness Challenge
Think of a different way to
express your gratitude than
saying "thank you" to
someone who helped you
and do it.

Date :   M T W T F S D
★   __ / __ / ____
Today I feel : (Circle one)
3 Things I am Thankful for :
The Best Time of my Day :   (Draw or Write)
Tomorrow will be Great because :
This Person brought me joy :
Positive Affirmation
« Giving makes me rich. »

Objective : Gratitude !

Make a list of all the things that help you feel better when you are sad : what are the things/ activities and people who comfort you? Share it with one of your parents if you feel like it and ask them about their tips for when they need comforting.

Date :
M T W T F S D
__ / __ / ____
Today I feel : (Circle one)
3 Things I am Thankful for :
The Best Time
of my Day :   (Draw or Write)
Tomorrow will be Great because :
This Person
brought me joy :
Inspiring Quote
« All things are difficult before being easy. »

Date :　**M T W T F S D**

★　　__ / __ / ____

Today I feel : (Circle one)

Date :
M T W T F S D
__ / __ / ____
Today I feel : (Circle one)
3 Things I am Thankful for :
The Best Time of my Day : (Draw or Write)
Tomorrow will be Great because :
This Person brought me joy :
Positive Affirmation
« Everyone has their own beliefs, I respect them. »

Date :
M T W T F S D
__ / __ / ____

Today I feel : (Circle one)

3 Things I am Thankful for :

The Best Time
of my Day :   (Draw or Write)

Tomorrow will be
Great because :

This Person
brought me joy :

Inspiring Quote
«Treat your body as your
friend: listen to your
sensations, these are the
messages it sends you. »

Date :
M T W T F S D
__ / __ / ____
Today I feel : (Circle one)
3 Things I am Thankful for :
The Best Time
of my Day :   (Draw or Write)
Tomorrow will be Great because :
This Person
brought me joy :
Positive Affirmation
« "I can change my behaviour to obtain different results.." »

Date : **M T W T F S D**

★ __ / __ / ____

3 Things I am Thankful for :

Date :　M T W T F S D

★　 __ / __ / ____

Today I feel : (Circle one)

3 Things I am Thankful for :

The Best Time
of my Day :　(Draw or Write)

Tomorrow will be Great because :

This Person
brought me joy :

Inspiring Quote

"Thank you" and "I love you" are magic formulas. »

Objective : Gratitude !

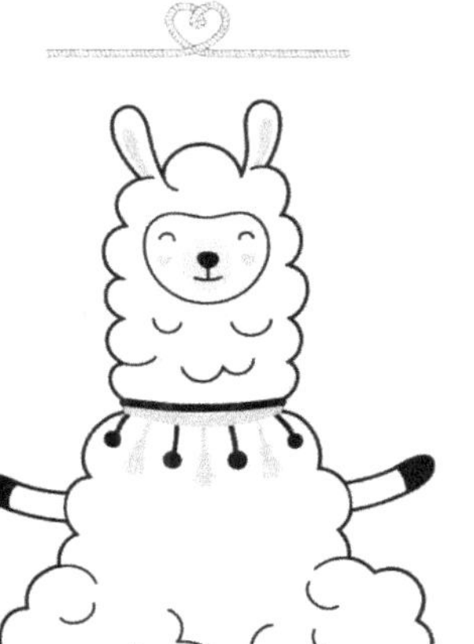

Activity

Describe your best achievement of the week.

How did it feel?

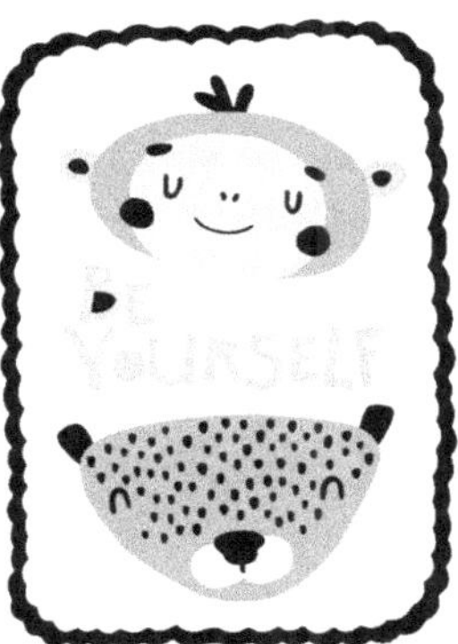

Date :   M T W T F S D
★   __ / __ / ____

Today I feel : (Circle one)

3 Things I am Thankful for :

The Best Time
of my Day :   (Draw or Write)

Tomorrow will be
Great because :

This Person
brought me joy :

Positive Affirmation
« I have the power to listen
without judging. »

Date :
M T W T F S D
__ / __ / ____
Today I feel : (Circle one)
3 Things I am Thankful for :
The Best Time
of my Day :   (Draw or Write)
Tomorrow will be
Great because :
This Person
brought me joy :
Kindness Challenge
Share some food you love
with someone you like.

Date : **M T W T F S D**

★ __ / __ / ____

Today I feel : (Circle one)

3 Things I am Thankful for :

The Best Time
of my Day :   (Draw or Write)

Tomorrow will be Great because :

This Person
brought me joy :

Inspiring Quote

"Listening relieves others. Being listened to is a relief."

Date :
M T W T F S D
__ / __ / ____
Today I feel : (Circle one)
3 Things I am Thankful for :
The Best Time
of my Day :   (Draw or Write)
Tomorrow will be Great because :
This Person
brought me joy :
Positive Affirmation
« I can go and immerse myself in Nature to recharge my batteries. »

Date :
M T W T F S D
★
__ / __ / ____
Today I feel : (Circle one)
3 Things I am Thankful for :
★
★
The Best Time
of my Day :   (Draw or Write)
★
Tomorrow will be Great because :
★
This Person
brought me joy :
Happiness Challenge
Put on your favorite song and dance! You can invite a friend to do it with you.
★

Date : **M T W T F S D**

★ __ / __ / ____

Today I feel : (Circle one)

3 Things I am Thankful for :

★

The Best Time
of my Day :   (Draw or Write)

Tomorrow will be Great because :

This Person
brought me joy :

Inspiring Quote

"if you want to change the world, start with yourself."

- Gandhi -

Date :   M T W T F S D
__ / __ / ____
Today I feel : (Circle one)
3 Things I am Thankful for :
The Best Time
of my Day :   (Draw or Write)
Tomorrow will be Great because :
This Person
brought me joy :
Positive Affirmation
« I have a kind heart. It feels good to be kind. »

Objective : Gratitude !

Activity

MADE WITH LOVE

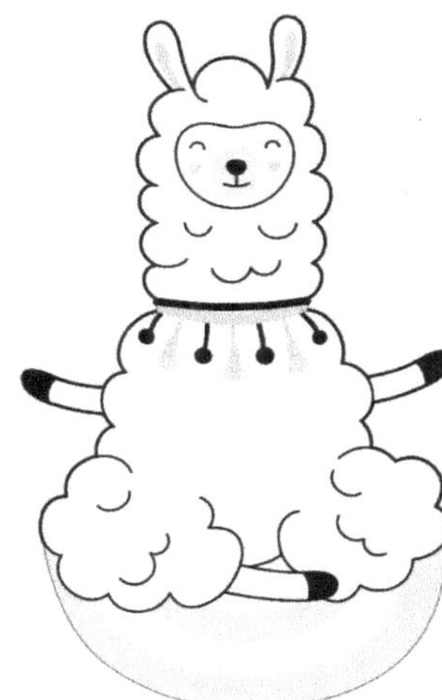

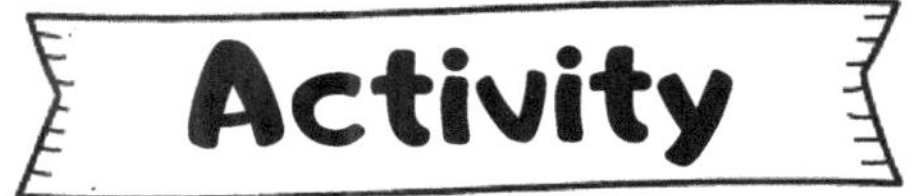

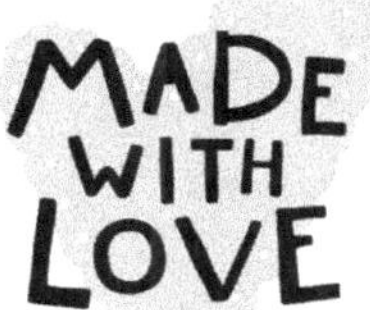

Draw what you prefer to do during vacations that makes you happy.

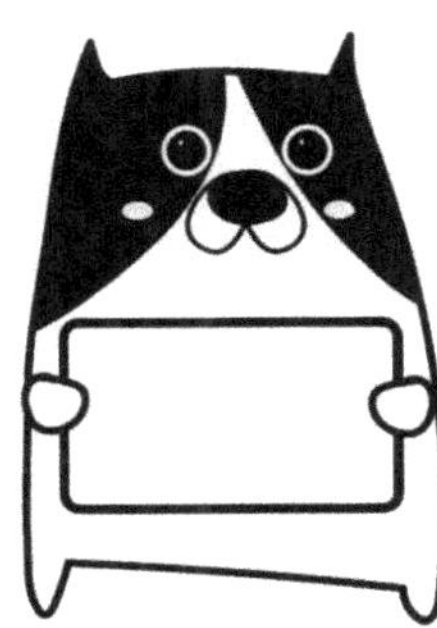

www.ingramcontent.com/pod-product-compliance
Lightning Source LLC
La Vergne TN
LVHW080520200726
843508LV00005B/1440